2001
Feb/March.

To
Dear Andrea

A memento of our wonderful holiday
in the South Island.
Much Love Alma x x x

Beautiful
south island
of new zealand

Beautiful **south** island
of new zealand

REED

Published by Reed Books, a division of Reed Publishing (NZ) Ltd, 39 Rawene Rd, Birkenhead, Auckland. Associated companies, branches and representatives throughout the world.

© 1997 Reed Publishing
ISBN 0 7900 0605 7
Reprinted 2000

The authors assert their moral rights in the work.

All photographs by Holger Leue unless otherwise acknowledged.

Front Cover: Ohinemaka Beach and Mt Strachan, South Westland by Nic Bishop
Previous page: Stewart Island
Back cover: Sheepdog memorial, Lake Tekapo; Penguin crossing sign, Oamaru; Cheese mural, Kaikoura

Designed by Sunny H. Yang

Printed by Everbest Printing Co.

Contents

The Marlborough Sounds offer glorious isolation, a calm haven in which to escape from the pressures of the world.

Marlborough and Nelson to Kaikoura

The Marlborough Sounds are magical sea-filled valleys which provide spectacular sailing and swimming. Their shores are clothed with unspoilt bush. Some of the islands further out are home to New Zealand's tuatara, a living link back to the dinosaurs of old.

Inland from the Sounds, the perspective changes. High tussock and alpine country overlook gentle river valleys and the sprawling Wairau Plains. Marlborough was once the home of great sheep stations, but today orchards, vineyards and berry fields dominate the landscape. The soil, and the sun, are particularly conducive to fine wine production and as a result Marlborough is home to some of New Zealand's best, and biggest, wineries.

West of Marlborough is Nelson, described by Abel Tasman in 1642 as 'a great land uplifted high'. Nelson shares with Blenheim one of the best climates in the country. Its beaches are golden sand swept by sparkling sea, the townships are colourful and friendly, and fruit trees, vines and berries flourish amid valleys of trees and ferns.

Nelson City, established by the New Zealand Company in 1842, is the centre of the province. Today it is a delightful mix of modernity and old world charm. Although its traditional industry remains horticulture, the area's rich fishing grounds have now turned Nelson into the biggest fishing port in New Zealand. The city is also a magnet for artisans — jewellers, potters, glassworkers and sculptors — who create some of New Zealand's finest craftworks. Close by is Abel Tasman National Park, a wonderful area of golden beaches, steep granite formations, limestone caves and native forest.

The Kaikoura coast follows the Pacific seaboard all the way down to Canterbury. Whaling was once a major industry along the coast. Today, the more gentle art of whalewatching provides an opportunity to witness some of the world's most beautiful creatures.

The hills surrounding the Marlborough Sounds are dotted with holiday homes, many of them reached by boat. During the still evenings the area is alive with the sounds of sea and forest. Among the most distinctive songsters of the region is the weka, a small flightless bird about the size of a domestic hen.

Lake Rotoroa, the larger of the two
lakes of Nelson Lakes National Park.

The sun, surf and wind make Abel
Tasman National Park ideal for
yachting, windsurfing and sea kayaking,
or simply lazing on its lovely beaches.

Many who visit Kaikoura come by train, enjoying the scenic coastal route. The area is famous for its kai moana, or seafood.

The view from Mount Fyffe, named
after a pioneer whaler. Today it is whale
watching that draws visitors to
Kaikoura, as well as adventure activities
such as paragliding.

Farmland falls to sea at Akaroa
Harbour, Banks Peninsula.

Christchurch and Canterbury

T he landscape of Canterbury is dominated by its mountains. They are sentinels of the southern sky, with passes like narrow gateways through to the West Coast. For the traveller they provide an everchanging vista of immense power and beauty. New Zealand's longest glacier, the Tasman, is located in Mt Cook National Park. Ski-planes regularly set down skiers at the top of the glacier for a fabulous run down a magical river of ice and snow.

The immense Canterbury Plains, once the home of the giant moa, seem to roll on forever. From the air, the plains look like a vast pastoral ocean of patchwork green and gold, interrupted every now and then by the blue-grey of an intricately braided river.

In 1840 the French established a settlement at Akaroa, on Banks Peninsula, a township which today still maintains a piquant Gallic flavour. But it wasn't until 1848 and the establishment of the Canterbury Association in London that the idea of founding an Anglican settlement in New Zealand was formulated. Two years later, in 1850, four ships — the *Randolph, Charlotte Jane, Cressy* and *Sir George Seymour* — landed at Lyttelton. The idea was to transpose a model English society, complete with bishop, gentry, tradespeople and other workers, people known for their respectability and high morals. The result was a South Seas version of Britain that has no parallel in New Zealand.

Nowhere is this more apparent than in Christchurch, the largest city of the South Island. The cathedral triumphs in the centre, and church spires spike the sky. Amid drifting willows the river Avon wends its way through a city of Gothic architecture and ever-changing colours. The green banks and parks blossom with flowers in spring, transforming the city into a colourful garden. Walk around the old university buildings, now transformed into an Arts Centre, or visit some of the city's older schools, splendid amid leafy settings, and you would think you were in an English university town.

There is, of course, also a 'new' Christchurch, vibrant and ambitious, which reminds you quite firmly that the city is looking very much to the future. A busy airport, a growing reputation as an industrial city utilising the best of modern technology, and progressive city planning have made Christchurch one of the most positive of New Zealand's cities.

Cambridge? No, punting on the River Avon, Kiwi-style. The river winds its way through the city of Christchurch, past the modern Town Hall with its ingenious fountain, and the nearby Floral Clock.

Christchurch's Cathedral Square is always alive with activity. Buskers entertain, people sit and watch the crowds pass by, and the city's Wizard declaims.

A prominent landmark in Lyttelton is
the Timeball Station, its Victorian
mechanism signalling the time to ships
in the harbour by the dropping of a ball
down the mast on the top of the tower.

Christ's College, founded on the principles of an English public school, is one of the country's oldest.

Two cyclists on Summit Road, the rim of the Port Hills, watch the sun set over Christchurch.

A large mural, painted on the side of the Fire Station at Lake Tekapo, acknowledges the place of sheep in the colourful history of the Mackenzie country.

The Church of the Good Shepherd, at
Lake Tekapo, was built in
acknowledgement of the sacrifices of the
early runholders of the area. The
sheepdogs of the Mackenzie country are
also honoured here.

Sheep graze on winter pasture beside
Lake Tekapo, South Canterbury.

Scenic flights over the Alps are popular.
A plane appears as a tiny speck of
colour above the vastness of the mighty
Tasman Glacier, and a helicopter lands
at the head of the glacier.

Mt Cook National Park covers 70,000
hectares of the Southern Alps, and 65
kilometres of mountain chains.

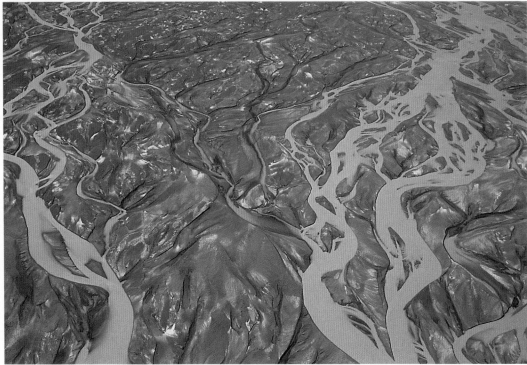

From the snow-capped peaks and
glaciers, water drains into the braided
rivers on both sides of the Main Divide,
and forms lakes such as Pukaki, a vital
part of the Upper Waitaki Power
Development Scheme.

A glimpse of what lies ahead, the
coastline of the West Coast.

The West Coast

The West Coast is rather like a forest fortress, its mountain peaks palisades guarding against all-comers. A constant curtain of rain provides an extra layer of protection. Were it not for the fabled greenstone, or pounamu, perhaps the Maori would never have come here, to the great Westland rivers, the Arahura and the Taramakau.

Later, another kind of stone, gold, brought Europeans into the area. Ironically, the gold was found beneath a greenstone boulder by Maori who were more interested in the pounamu. This was in 1864. A year later gold mining began in Hokitika and Reefton. Even later, another mineral, coal, added to the region's prosperity.

The goldmining days brought a sense of the frontier to the West Coast. Perhaps it is because of this that Coasters are considered different from other New Zealanders. Not any better or worse, just a bit different — irreverent, enterprising, sometimes stubborn, but always decent. In many respects they are the archetypal 'good keen men' and independent women of New Zealand's ideal society, having a healthy disrespect for authority and relying more on their own sense of what's right and what isn't.

One of the most dominant features of the West Coast is the opalescent sea, which seems to carry on a constant love affair with the coast. The whole of the West Coast is a place of whispers, of sounds and mysteries, offering moments of sheer beauty as when a white heron feathers the air at its nesting place at Okarito.

It is also a place of immense silence. The beaches are unpopulated and the emerald green forests are isolated. Nowhere is the silence more profound than at the two rivers of ice — the Fox and Franz Josef Glaciers. Sometimes, in the gleaming half-light of day, they defy reality and render the surrounding landscape unreal also.

The astonishing Pancake Rocks, at
Punakaiki, lie within one of New
Zealand's newest national parks,
Paparoa. Nearby the rich red of the
pohutukawa flower adds a vivid splash
of colour to the bush. A little further
south, a cyclist sets out on the road to
adventure.

During the latter part of the nineteenth century Okarito was alive with pubs, dance halls, casinos, banks and stores, as miners flocked to join the search for gold on the Coast. Today it is a quieter place, sought for its detachment from the world, and the allure of its whitebait.

A canoeist shares the peace of Okarito
Lagoon with a rare white heron, or
kotuku. The only breeding ground of
the kotuku is on the banks of the
nearby Waitangiroto Stream.

Guided walking tours take visitors right
on to the magnificent Fox and Franz
Josef Glaciers. At close quarters these
shining rivers of ice ripple with blue and
green colours and reveal jumbled blocks
of ice.

Gillespies Beach is part of a rocky coast
that was once part of the gold rushes,
and the allure of the precious metal still
calls back resolute goldpanners.

The West Coast combines superb
natural beauty with an immense
diversity of flora — some of the species
in Westland National Park date back
over 160 million years.

The perfect reflections of Westland's
Lake Matheson in early morning light.

The West Coast is renowned for its extraordinary weather and skyscapes. Cloud swirls over Mt Tasman (below), and a rainbow emerges after a shower (right).

Winter landscape near Lindis Pass.

Dunedin and Otago

Otago is a place of mountains, lakes and glaciers. Most striking are The Remarkables, near Queenstown, but equally lovely are the mountains around Lakes Hawea, Wanaka and Wakatipu, where glaciers ground the hills into rounded shapes before the time of man. Then there is the Clutha, a river of immense strength, storming through steep gorges to the sea.

Queenstown is New Zealand's best-known mountain resort. An area of unsurpassable beauty, it is also a centre for adventure activities — jetboating, rafting, tramping, heliskiing or, for those who don't mind being tied by the ankles, the ultimate thrill — bungy jumping.

The earliest Europeans in Otago were whalers. As with Christchurch, however, settlers soon realised the potential of the alluvial plains, and in 1848 the ships *John Wickliffe* and *Philip Laing*, with three hundred settlers aboard, arrived in Otago Harbour. Primarily Presbyterian, the Scottish founders established Dunedin on the fortunes of great sheep stations. The discovery of gold boosted the city's coffers and, by 1871, one in every four settlers in New Zealand was to be found in Otago. By the 1880s Dunedin was the country's largest, most industrialised and pre-eminent commercial city. Although this is not the situation today, Dunedin still exerts considerable influence nationally.

Dunedin has the reputation of being the Edinburgh of the South, the result of its Scottish heritage. Constructed of grey stone, it is a handsome city, with many buildings that are perfect Victorian artefacts. Everywhere there are church spires topping churches of austere Gothic grandeur. The Municipal Chambers display a frontage in the Italian style, while the architecture of the law courts, the railway station and the university attest to a Victorian exuberance muted by a sense of respectability.

Throughout Otago there are still signs of a prosperity based on whaling, sheep rearing and gold. Otago's greatest treasure, though, is its unique landscape.

Lake Wanaka (above and centre left) and Lake Hawea (bottom left) are water-filled glaciated valleys, the result of glacier action that has smoothed and rounded the landscape below the surrounding peaks.

Rosehips and willows grace the
Matukituki river valley.

Mustering time at Loch Linnhe Station,
near Queenstown. Meanwhile, on the
banks of Lake Wakatipu, sheep briefly
take precedence on the road.

Queenstown is the home of adventure,
with bungy jumping and jet boating two
of its major attractions.

If a jump from the historic Kawarau
Bridge doesn't appeal, you can take a
gondola ride up to Bobs Peak, high
above Queenstown.

60

TSS *Earnslaw* is the last of four steamers that plied Lake Wakatipu during the height of the gold rush days. Queenstown nestles on the edge of the lake.

A sea lion, glistening sovereign of the seashore, roars at Moeraki Peninsula. The Moeraki coastline is steeped in Maori history, and the famed Moeraki boulders, each weighing several tonnes, are said to be the petrified food baskets of an early canoe which was wrecked on the offshore reef.

Taiaroa Head is the home of a famous
Royal Albatross colony. Also on the
Otago Peninsula is the imposing Otakou
Marae. A scenic rail journey in this part
of New Zealand must take in the craggy
Taieri Gorge.

The University of Otago was the first university in New Zealand. The old part of the building was begun in 1870.

Larnach's Castle, built in 1871 by a wealthy banker who later became a Member of Parliament, is notable for its impressive ballroom, ornate ceilings and Italian marble fireplaces.

Dunedin Railway Station, built in 1907, is embellished with an impressive tower, magnificent mosaic floor, and stained glass windows with a distinctly 'railways' theme.

Olveston is an Edwardian residence that conjures up the elegance of a bygone era, beautifully furnished with antiques, fine paintings and memorabilia.

Lush ferns in a remote Fiordland
setting.

Murihiku: The South

The southern end of Aotearoa is known to the Maori as Murihiku, and encompasses Southland, Fiordland and Stewart Island. Southland's history is similar to that of Otago. Invercargill was settled by Scots people from Dunedin in 1856, and the Scots heritage is still noticeable in the way Southlanders speak; there is a distinct burr on their r's. The new settlers found Southland similar to the Scottish highlands, and they established sheep runs on the Southland plains.

Bluff is the harbour from which agricultural produce is sent to all parts of the globe. It is also a vigorous fishing port, with catches of deep-sea fish, crayfish and shellfish. The Bluff oyster is considered by connoisseurs to be the ultimate in oysters.

Offshore from Invercargill is Stewart Island, a special place of bush-clad hills and quiet beaches. The Maori name is Rakiura, a reference to the glowing skies and auroras which play on the southern horizon.

West of Invercargill the vista opens out to the unparalleled beauty of Fiordland National Park. Sea and the massive forces of the Ice Ages have created astounding physical configurations to the land. Every day rain, wind, cloud and sleet combine to recreate an everchanging panorama. Along the coast are the great fiords — Milford, Bligh, Caswell, Nancy, Doubtful, Dusky and Preservation Inlet. Inland are the Takitimu Mountains and the lakes Te Anau and Manapouri, and the magnificent Milford Track, a walk which has been called the finest in the world.

The superb Catlins coast has a rugged
grandeur that, once experienced, is
never forgotten.

Nugget Point lighthouse surveys a rocky
coast. In contrast, the small church at
Waikawa is serene in the sunshine.

Sheep shearing is a fast and furious business — definitely not for the faint-hearted.

A field of wild flowers on the road to Milford Sound. Milford is dominated by Mitre Peak, rising steeply from the deep waters of the fiord.

Trampers experience all types of conditions on the 54-kilometre Milford Track, often described as 'the finest walk in the world'. The magnificent Bowen Falls drop down into Milford Sound.

Dawn at Cascade Cove, Dusky Sound,
and half-light at Acheron Passage.

Doubtful Sound, named Doubtfull
Harbour by Captain Cook in 1770, is
one of the most haunting of the
numerous southern fiords. Nearby,
morning mist hovers over the rainforest.

A playful dolphin leaps before the Milford Wanderer, scouting across the mist-shrouded waters of Dusky Sound.

No matter where you are, you will
always find surfers chasing the waves,
even here at Oreti Beach, among the
most southern waves of the world.

The tuatara, often called New Zealand's
living dinosaur. Southland Museum in
Invercargill has the country's most
successful breeding programme.

In Bluff, at the very bottom of the South
Island, Fred and Myrtle Flutey have
turned their house into a showcase for
the paua shell.

Stewart Island is a special place. Remote and sparsely populated, it has great appeal to trampers and others seeking peace and tranquillity. It also supports a vigorous fishing industry.

Acknowledgements

Thank you to the many New Zealanders who welcomed me to Aotearoa and made me feel at home.

And thank you, friends and fellow travellers, for the inspiration and the best of times. You know who you are.

— H.L.

Thanks to Montana Wines Ltd and Air New Zealand for travel assistance in the South Island, and to Holger Leue, Ian Watt, Susan Brierley, Chris Lipscombe and Alison Jacobs.

— W.I.